BASKETBALL LEGENDS

Kareem Abdul-Jabbar

Larry Bird

WITHDRAWN

Wilt Chamberlain

Julius Erving

Magic Johnson

Michael Jordan

CHELSEA HOUSE PUBLISHERS

BASKETBALL LEGENDS

LARRY BIRD

33

Sean Dolan

Introduction by
Chuck Daly

CHELSEA HOUSE PUBLISHERS
New York · Philadelphia

Produced by Daniel Bial Agency
New York, New York.

Picture research by Alan Gottlieb
Cover illustration by Daniel O'Leary

First Printing

1 3 5 7 9 8 6 4 2

Dolan, Sean.
    Larry Bird / Sean Dolan.
      p. cm. — (Basketball legends)
    Includes bibliographical references and index.
    ISBN 0-7910-2427-X (hard) $14.95
    1. Bird, Larry, 1956– —Juvenile literature. 2. Basketball players—
    United States—Biography—Juvenile literature. [1. Bird, Larry, 1956–.
    2. Basketball players.] I. Title. II. Series.
    GV884.B57D65 1994
    796.323'092—dc20
    [B]   94-5776
                                                                CIP
                                                                AC

CONTENTS

BECOMING A
BASKETBALL LEGEND

Chuck Daly

What does it take to be a basketball superstar? Two of the three things it takes are easy to spot. Any great athlete must have excellent skills and tremendous dedication. The third quality needed is much harder to define, or even put in words. Others call it leadership or desire to win, but I'm not sure that explains it fully. This third quality relates to the athlete's thinking process, a certain mentality and work ethic. One can coach athletic skills, and while few superstars need outside influence to help keep them dedicated, it is possible for a coach to offer some well-timed words in order to keep that athlete fully motivated. But a coach can do no more than appeal to a player's will to win; how much that player is then capable of ensuring victory is up to his own internal workings.

In recent times, we have been fortunate to have seen some of the best to play the game. Larry Bird, Magic Johnson, and Michael Jordan had all three components of superstardom in full measure. They brought their teams to numerous championships, and made the players around them better. (They also made their coaches look smart.)

I myself coached a player who belongs in that class, Isiah Thomas, who helped lead the Detroit Pistons to consecutive NBA crowns. Isiah is not tall—he's just over six feet—but he could do whatever he wanted with the ball. And what he wanted to do most was lead and win.

All the players I mentioned above and those whom this

series will chronicle are tremendously gifted athletes, but for the most part, you can't play professional basketball at all unless you have excellent skills. And few players get to stay on their team unless they are willing to dedicate themselves to improving their talents even more, learning about their opponents, and finding a way to join with their teammates and win.

It's that third element that separates the good player from the superstar, the memorable players from the legends of the game. Superstars know when to take over the game. If the situation calls for a defensive stop, the superstars stand up and do it. If the situation calls for a key pass, they make it. And if the situation calls for a big shot, they want the ball. They don't want the ball simply because of their own glory or ego. Instead they know—and their teammates know—that they are the ones who can deliver, regardless of the pressure.

The words "legend" and "superstar" are often tossed around without real meaning. Taking a hard look at some of those who truly can be classified as "legends" can provide insight into the things that brought them to that level. All of them developed their legacy over numerous seasons of play, even if certain games will always stand out in the memories of those who saw them. Those games typically featured amazing feats of all-around play. No matter how great the fans thought the superstars, the players were capable yet of surprising them, their opponents, and occasionally even themselves. The desire to win took over, and with their dedication and athletic skills already in place, they were capable of the most astonishing achievements.

CHUCK DALY, most recently the head coach of the New Jersey Nets, guided the Detroit Pistons to two straight NBA championships, in 1989 and 1990. He earned a gold medal as coach of the 1992 U.S. Olympic basketball team—the so-called "Dream Team"—and was inducted into the Pro Basketball Hall of Fame in 1994.

1

STEAL OF THE CENTURY

As always on the basketball court, he was thinking. This time, he was literally on the basketball court, having had his shot blocked and been knocked to the ground. His teammates scrambled to save the ball, to no avail. Detroit had the ball, the lead, and only five seconds remained on the clock.

"The primary thing I was thinking," Larry Bird recollected later, "was 'Get up!' Because there was still time to do *something.*"

It was the fifth and most likely decisive game of the 1987 Eastern Conference Finals playoff series between the Boston Celtics and the Detroit Pistons. Old, injured, and weary, the defending NBA champion Celtics were facing a tremendous challenge from a Pistons team that was young, deep, relentless, and very hungry. For almost eight years now, as long as their star forward Larry Bird had been in the

Larry Bird drives around Detroit's Adrian Dantley in Game 2 of the 1987 playoffs. Bird scored 31 points as the Celtics took a 2-0 series lead.

league, Boston had dominated the Eastern Conference, reaching the conference finals seven times and winning the NBA title on three of those occasions, but the Pistons were convinced they could end the Celtics' reign.

At first glance, the Detroit challenge seemed unlikely to succeed. Boston had won a conference-best 59 games in the regular season, seven more than Detroit. Its starting five was one of the best of all time and featured, besides Bird, two other certain future hall-of-famers: center Robert Parish and forward Kevin McHale. Parish had made the All-Star game for the seventh straight time that year; guard Dennis Johnson had made the league's all-defensive team for the ninth year in a row. McHale had averaged 26 points a game while shooting a phenomenal 60 percent from the floor; the often overlooked Danny Ainge was one of the league's most deadly three-point shooters.

Bird, three times the league's most valuable player and the generally acknowledged best all-around player in the game, had just enjoyed one of the greatest regular seasons of his career, amassing career highs in assists, field goal percentage, and minutes played, leading the league in free throw percentage, and averaging 28.1 points, 9.2 rebounds, and 6.6 assists per game.

Coming off three straight trips to the NBA finals, the Celtics were unquestionably the league's nobility, and carried themselves with a lordly arrogance. No one epitomized that attitude more than the proud and occasionally quickfisted Bird, who with his myriad skills was also a master of oncourt verbal intimidation. "I guess I try to carry myself a certain way on the court," acknowledged the NBA's consensus champion trashtalker, who had been described on more than one occasion as "the meanest son of a bitch in the league" by his admiring coach and respectful opponents. "When you lose that, you've got nothing."

But the Pistons respected no opponent, no matter what their level of achievement. Though they could not hope to match Boston's distinguished hoops pedigree—there was not a championship ring among them, and Isiah Thomas, their wondrous point guard and best player, had played in just 22 playoff games in his entire career, compared to Bird's 115—the Pistons under the leadership of their coach, Chuck Daly, had been transformed from perennial doormats to the league's bullies. Styling themselves the Bad Boys and reveling in their outlaw image, the big, belligerent, vocal and rough Pistons had become the best defensive, most physical, least liked team in the league, and they backed down from no one.

So for all Boston's undeniable greatness and justified pride, there was good reason for Detroit's belief, in Bird's words, that "they were definitely good enough to beat us." Detroit entered the series rested and healthy, while Boston was weary and aching. Celtic players had missed a staggering total of 206 games due to injury in the regular season, and the problem had worsened in the playoffs. Key frontcourt reserve Bill Walton, himself a future hall-of-famer, was completely unavailable, and McHale and Parish were both hobbling with severe ankle injuries. And among the career highs Bird had amassed in the regular season was an ominous one: eight games missed, due to a chronic back problem that would ultimately end his career.

The result was that the cocky Pistons were well aware of what Bird would only later concede: that by this point in the season he was "just not the same player" he had been earlier, just as the Celtics "just weren't the same team we had been the year before," when they had won a remarkable 67 regular-season games and the NBA championship.

Boston retained one advantage, however: its home court. By virtue of their superior regular-season record, the Celtics would play four of the possible seven games with the Pistons at home in the Boston Garden, where they were virtually invincible, having won 34 of their last 35 games and beaten Detroit 14 straight times. On the road, however, the Celtics' weaknesses had begun to show: they had dropped 14 of their last 18 regular-season contests away from home, and they privately conceded that their only real chance to beat the Pistons was to take all four games in Boston.

Nothing that happened in the first four games of the series did anything to alter either team's assessment of the situation. The Celtics squeezed out wins in games one and two in Boston, but the Pistons destroyed them in games three and four back at the Pontiac Silverdome, their cavernous suburban home stadium, winning by 18 and 26 points. Though the series was just even, the Pistons were clearly quicker, stronger, faster, deeper, and fresher, and the Celtics were surviving only on guts, guile, and experience. Moreover, Detroit's confrontational style had succeeded in provoking the Celtics and throwing them off their game; the Celtics seemed distracted and unfocused, as interested in retaliating for every Detroit cheap shot as they were in playing basketball—exactly the kind of on-court atmosphere the Pistons sought to create.

Even Bird, the Celtics' captain and the team's heart and soul, was having problems. Checked by an incredibly agile, indefatigable rookie named Dennis Rodman, he was having a terrible time getting good shots; never had he looked so slow and vulnerable on the hardwood. Shockingly, in the third contest, he had completely lost his composure and been ejected from the game after throwing several punches at Bill Laimbeer, Detroit's provocative center, after an unnecessarily hard foul. So as the Celtics took the famous parquet floor of the Boston Garden for game five, they were more desperate than ever to retain their home-court advantage, for they would have to go back to Pontiac without Parish, who had been suspended for the sixth contest for clubbing the villainous Laimbeer to the floor with his fists in game four. And the Pistons did not want to wait for a deciding game seven to break the hex Boston held on them in the Garden, for in the Celtics' illustrious history, in which they had won twice as many championships (16) as the next nearest franchise, they had never lost a

In Game 3 of the 1987 series, Bill Laimbeer's hard foul provoked Larry Bird into a fight. The ejection of both players meant an advantage for the Detroit Pistons.

seventh game, let alone one played at home.

The Celtics raced out to a 12-point lead in the second quarter, but the Pistons' characteristically rugged defense brought them back, and with 6:40 left to play in the contest, they held a five-point advantage. With their aging starters having played virtually every minute, the Celtics appeared to be out of gas.

Then, as he had done so many times in the past, Bird demonstrated why he had earned the simple sobriquet "the Legend." With him keying the rally with his customary precision long-range shooting and pinpoint passing, the Celtics took a 100-99 lead with just over two minutes remaining. The two teams exchanged baskets; then Bird, with Pistons draped all over him, hit a fallaway jumper from deep in the corner to give the Celtics a three-point lead with only a minute to play. But the Pistons would not go away. As the suddenly quiet Boston crowd watched in disbelief, Laimbeer and then Thomas scored for Detroit, giving the Pistons a one-point edge with just 17 seconds remaining.

Both teams, their coaches, the thousands of fans in the arena, and the millions more watching on television knew where Boston would go for its final shot, for Bird's last-second heroics were the most enduring lore in his legend. "I fear no man on the basketball court—except Larry Bird," Earvin "Magic" Johnson, who was then Bird's only rival for the title of the game's best all-around player, once said. "Because if there's any time left on that clock, he'll find a way to beat you." Bird reveled in such moments, to the point of often making bold on-court predictions of his gamewinning feats. "I get a charge out of telling someone on the opposing team that I'm going to hit a last-second shot and then doing it. That's what it's all about," he once said; but this time, as Boston broke its timeout huddle and returned to the floor, the Legend was silent, perhaps in recognition of all that was at stake.

Bird got the ball on the left side of the floor, beyond the three-point line, and looked up at the burly but slow Rick Mahorn, who had switched to him when Rodman got lost in a thicket of Celtic picks. An almost imperceptible ball and shoulder fake froze Mahorn and Bird whipped around him. As he neared the hoop, the 6'9" forward noticed Dennis Rodman and another Piston converging on him, and laid the ball up toward the glass.

To Bird's surprise, Rodman leaped and smacked the shot out of the air before it could reach the backboard. There was contact, but no foul, and Bird was knocked to the floor, where he watched several teammates scramble unsuccessfully after the bounding basketball.

Detroit ball, five seconds left. On the Boston bench, Walton dropped his head into his hands, and the team's coach, K. C. Jones, turned stoically away. On the court, the Pistons' players, ignoring their coach's frantic signals for a time-out, were leaping up and down and embracing, celebrating their victory and the likely end of the Boston dynasty. All Detroit had to do was inbound the ball. "The game was over, and Detroit had won," Jones later remembered thinking.

Lying on the parquet floor, Bird saw the chaos on the court: A Boston player who had chased the ball into the stands was still extricating himself from the crowd; on the left side-

Bird is mobbed after making the "Steal of the Century."

line, Thomas was begging the referee to hand him the basketball so he could pass it in to one of his teammates before the distraught Celtics could regroup. With both teams in disarray, Bird hauled himself up and ran to the foul line toward Detroit guard Joe Dumars, the most likely target for Thomas's pass.

Thomas looked instead to Laimbeer, who was standing just inside the lane, almost under the Boston basket, unguarded—or so it seemed, for Bird had identified the Piston center as Thomas's target in the same instant that the Detroit star had, and had begun moving toward him, unnoticed, before the ball even left

Thomas's hand. "Other players might think two or three plays ahead," Magic Johnson once said. "Larry Bird thinks five minutes ahead."

Once out of Thomas's hand, the ball "seemed to hang there forever," said Bird, who darted in front of Laimbeer, slapped the ball away (starting the clock), and controlled it as he tightroped along the left baseline with his back to the basket. He thought about trying to get his feet into position to take a desperation last shot, but instead he quickly yet seemingly unhurriedly turned, spotted a "white blur" cutting hard to the basket, and delivered a perfect pass to the streaking Dennis Johnson, who with Dumars on his back laid the ball up and in with his left hand for a stunning Celtics victory as the buzzer sounded and the Pistons looked around in disbelief.

In its combination of resilience, poise, nerve, intelligence, physical grace, timing, and teamwork, the miraculous play epitomized perfectly the Bird legend. "Steal of the Century" read the headline on the *Boston Herald* the next day, but one observer downplayed the moment's greatness. The play was "easy," said Boston assistant coach Chris Ford, "because he's Larry Bird." But no one, except for Bird himself, knew in truth how difficult it really all had been.

2
DOWN IN THE VALLEY

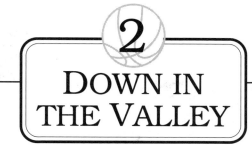

Larry Joe Bird was born on December 7, 1956, in Bedford, Indiana. He was the fourth child and third son born to Joe and Georgia Kerns Bird. From his mother, Larry would inherit his height—Georgia was six feet tall—and looks; from his father, a belief in physical toughness and stoicism as virtues; from both, a stubborn and sensitive pride.

When it came time to take her newborn son home, Georgia Bird needed help carrying him, both because she was still weak from her pregnancy and because the blond infant was so large—11 pounds 12 ounces at birth. Larry performed amazing feats of strength and physical coordination at an early age. He could push himself up at just three months, stand alone at seven months, and walk at nine months. By a year he was too strong and physically independent to sleep in a crib any longer; he had

As a junior in high school, Bird was able to palm the ball easily. At right is friend and teammate Tony Clark.

destroyed two of them, as well as a playpen, and he was put to sleep each night in a regular bed that he shared with his two older brothers.

The Bird home at the time of Larry's birth was in the tiny town of West Baden, in Orange County, Indiana, one of many rundown, too-small houses the family would rent in the first 12 years of Larry's life. In the first 18 years of Joe and Georgia's marriage, the Birds would live in 17 different rented houses, often leaving just one step ahead of the rent collectors, sometimes with the children hauling the family's furniture down the street on their little red wagons.

The house Larry lived in during the 1970s. As a kid, Larry often visited his grandmother's house—partly to avoid the chaos at home, and partly because she lived across from public basketball courts.

With the much bigger town of French Lick and tiny Prospect, West Baden constitutes what its residents refer to as "the valley." Orange County, which is in the southwest part of Indiana, was the poorest county in the state. The predominantly rural valley, home to just a few thousand people, was the poorest part of the county, and the Birds were among the poorest families in the valley.

"In Orange County," explains a resident to Lee Daniel Levine, a Bird biographer, "you work hard and you die young." Joe Bird had grown up one of twelve kids in a family remarkable both for its poverty—other residents of the valley habitually sewed clothes for the Bird children from the material of their own children's outgrown outfits—and the character of his

mother, Helen, who was generally acknowledged to be the meanest woman in the valley, if
not in the entire county. Joe Bird saw combat
in both World War II and the Korean War.
Though he never spoke of his years in the
service, the symptoms of what today is called
post-traumatic stress disorder were clear:
nightmares, flashbacks, nervous irritability,
eruptions of violent anger. Friends remember
him diving for cover at the sound of loud
noises, as if a shell had gone off nearby. Those
same friends remember him, as does Larry, as
funny, warm-hearted, physically tough, and
incredibly generous with what little he had, but
Joe would also have flashbacks during which
he would batter his wife, who understood, she
later said, that in those violent moments she
had become the "enemy."

Joe's constant drinking and resistance to
authority made it hard for him to hold a job for
very long. The burden of holding the family
together therefore fell to Georgia. Though
plagued throughout her adult life by severe
migraine headaches, she usually worked two
jobs, most often in a shoe factory, on a chicken
farm, as an aide at a nursing home, or as a
waitress.

Though Georgia's hard work kept her family
alive, the Birds would never, in Larry's child-
hood, be prosperous. Larry never had a tele-
phone in any of the many houses he grew up
in, for example, but that was not a great hardship. There was often, even in the dead of the
cold Indiana winters, no heat or electricity,
either, and relatives got in the habit of leaving
milk and food in the Birds' refrigerator whenever they visited. In a typical week, Bird has said,

his mother would work almost 100 hours for take-home pay of $100, only to face a minimum weekly grocery bill of $120 to feed her brood of large, athletic, hungry kids.

When Larry was 13, the family was finally able to scrape together $200 for a down payment on a house. The Birds' new address was in French Lick, but Larry's excitement about the move quickly came to an end when he learned that their new home was the "haunted house" where he had always been afraid to deliver papers on his newspaper route. Its ramshackle, spooky appearance, crumbled porch, and saggy doorframes made it look "as if ghosts were living there," he said in his autobiography, *Drive.*

At school, the Bird children were teased because of their clothes and low social status. But by the time he was a teenager, Larry Bird had discovered a way to stop the others from laughing and pay him a more positive kind of attention: basketball.

It is the rare male in Indiana who is not exposed to the sport at a young age, for in that state basketball is embraced with a passion unknown anywhere else in the United States. Eighteen of the world's twenty largest high-school gymnasiums are in Indiana, and in many towns the high-school gym is often a larger, more up-to-date facility than the school to which it is attached. Such gyms invariably have a seating capacity much larger than the student body of the school itself and often larger than the population of the entire town. In many of the state's small towns, the high school basketball coach is often one of the most important citizens, and the highlight of every winter is the state basketball tournament, in which every school in the state competes, without differentiation as to size. "In Indiana, we don't watch or play basketball," sportswriter Bob Collins of the *Indianapolis Star* has written. "We live it, breathe it, taste it, smell it, sleep it."

Larry Bird received his first basketball as a Christmas gift when he was four years old. Athletic, like all the Birds (Joe had been a superb basketball player until he dropped out of school in the eighth grade to go to work), Larry was always tagging along with his older brothers, and his basketball always went with him. By the age of eight, he was spending much of his time at the home of his grandmother Lizzie Kerns in French Lick, and she learned to recognize his arrival by the thump-thump of his basketball as he dribbled along.

Even by Indiana standards young Larry Bird's devotion to the game was extraordinary. Though he received exceptional coaching at a very young age due to the area's highly developed youth basketball programs, it was the long hours he put in on his own that made him special as a player.

Even when he was very young, Larry was relentlessly driven on the court: emotional, outspoken, intelligent, intuitive, reckless, a leader. "His [basketball] instinct was always there," Gary Holland, one of his first coaches remembered, as was an unyielding competitiveness, honed from the endless fraternal contests with his two older brothers. "Those brothers were so competitive, and they just pounded on the kid," said Jim Jones, who coached Larry as a very young player and later in high school. "Boy, he'd fight them tooth and nail, and he'd stay around and play after they'd leave."

Residents of French Lick soon grew accustomed to hearing—even late at night, long after the games had stopped and the other players had gone home, sometimes even at one or two in the morning—the rhythmic thud of a basketball against the pavement and seeing a tall, skinny, blond kid shooting in the schoolyard by himself. "I never saw a kid who played basketball so much," Holland says simply.

Off the court, Larry was laconic, withdrawn, moody, private, suspicious, and proud—very like his mother. On the court, he was something else entirely.

Bird's game began to come together when he was 14 and a rail-thin—at 6'1", he weighed just 131 pounds—sophomore guard on the Springs Valley High School junior varsity team. Just two games into the season, Bird broke his left ankle going for a rebound. The injury kept him out of games, but it did not keep him from working out. Recruiting younger kids from the neighborhood to rebound for him, he intensified his shooting drills, firing away while propped up on his crutches. An unexceptional shooter to that point, he found, when his ankle healed, that he suddenly seemed to be making all his shots. "Then one day—I can remember it exactly—I started making everything," Bird recalled. "After that, the older guys chose me first."

While recuperating, Bird also worked tirelessly on his passing. He fired the ball again and again against whatever surface—a wall, a fence, some chairs placed on the court—would return it to him. The result was a perfection not only of his ballhandling technique but the development of the uncanny on-court vision that would be the most singular feature of his multifaceted game. Now, not only did Bird exhibit perfect form in his passing, but he could *see* things, *anticipate* things in the eternally-shifting geometry of 10 players in constant motion on the court, that others simply could not. What he had discovered, he said, was nothing less than "a whole new way to play." Once he was able to play competitively again, Bird said, "I began throwing these fantastic passes like I had never thrown before. I have no idea where it came from, but there it was. I remember being in the locker room after the first day back and guys saying, 'God, Larry, where did you learn to pass like that?'"

To make the metamorphosis complete, Bird experienced a most welcome late-adolescent growth spurt. As a junior, he was still only 6'2", but by his senior year, he had sprouted up to 6'7". Because he grew so late, until his senior year Bird had played guard throughout his basketball career and had honed, at an exceptional level, the "little man's" skills of dribbling, passing, and outside shooting; as he grew, he was also to become a dominating rebounder and inside player.

As Bird matured physically, he became a player with an unprecedented combination of size, strength, and shooting and ballhandling

As a junior, Bird led his high school team to a 19-2 record, although the year was marred by an unexpected loss in the sectional finals of the state tournament.

skills. Occasionally he was criticized for being slow afoot or not a good jumper—but he more than offset these physical limitations with his supreme grasp of positioning and other fundamentals, his excellence and creativity as a shooter and passer, and, most of all, his preternatural court awareness and focus. Nobody ever played harder than Bird, and no one ever played smarter.

As a junior, Bird was not the high scorer on the Springs Valley team. Then, as always, he preferred passing, he said, which "is more of an art than scoring." Still, he was its best all-around player, averaging 16 points, 10 rebounds, and 6 assists per game.

As a senior, Bird, playing center, increased his production to 30.6 points, 20.6 rebounds, and 4.3 assists per game and set valley single-game records for points (55) and rebounds (38). Though the team was upset in the regional final of the state tournament, the premature end to the season could not detract from the magnificence of his performance.

In 1974, Springs Valley High won the sectional championship. Bird was hurt by not being named to the Associated Press's first or second All-State teams, but said later, "Maybe it worked out for the best. It kept me practicing four or five hours a day."

Remarkably, Bird was not named to the Associated Press's first or second All-State teams, and he was the very last selection for the Indiana all-star team that was picked for the annual home-and-home series with the best high-school players from neighboring Kentucky, a state nearly as basketball-mad as

Indiana. Journalists and coaches tended to be skeptical about the level of athletic competition in southern Indiana: it was assumed that players from the rural regions of the southern part of the state were seldom equal to those from more urban areas. To make matters worse for Bird, he mainly rode the bench against the Kentucky all-stars, even though he had clearly been one of the team's best players in practice.

Bird quickly narrowed his choices for higher education to three in-state schools: Indiana University (IU), Indiana State University, and Purdue University. He also kept a fourth option open as well: not attending college at all. At that time, he considered a professional career a remote possibility at best, and wondered if he could better help his family by going to work.

Everyone expected Bird to choose Indiana University, which had one of the greatest basketball traditions in the country. To be offered a scholarship by Bobby Knight, the most celebrated and important individual in the entire state, was the dream of virtually every young hoopster in the state. Bird himself seemed to prefer Indiana State, but his father and brothers were huge IU fans. Only Georgia Bird had reservations: she disliked Coach Knight's domineering, abusive style, and she believed as well that her favorite son, who was almost a year younger than most of the students in his grade, was still too young to leave home.

Typically closemouthed, Bird did not reveal the stress he was feeling to anyone, but in the evening before Knight was to visit French Lick, he cried and admitted to his mother, "I don't really want to go to IU. But I guess I'd let too many people down if I don't."

3
BIRTH OF A LEGEND

After just 24 days at IU, with barely a word to anyone let alone Coach Knight, Bird walked out to Highway 37, stuck out his thumb, and hitchhiked back to the valley. He had not even lasted until the opening of basketball practice.

Life in Bloomington at IU was overwhelming—the school's student body enrollment of 33,000 was more than 16 times the population of French Lick—and Bird felt out of place there academically and socially.

The basketball court was no longer the refuge it had once been for him. Incredible as it now seems, Bird had been recruited essentially as an afterthought by Knight, when a scholarship opened up at the last moment. The team's upperclassmen constituted an extraordinary squad that over the next two years would lose just one game and win a national champi-

Larry Bird's passing ability could amaze a teammate (Alex Gilbert, right) as much as an opponent (DePaul University's James Mitchem, left).

onship, so even in informal pick-up games before the official start of practice on October 15, Bird was rarely picked to play.

With a team so obviously talented, Knight had little inclination to concern himself with the adjustment problems of a relatively unheralded freshman. "When Bird left," Knight remembered years later, "we hadn't even noticed. It was like 'the hell with him.'"

Back in French Lick, Bird found himself scarcely more welcome than he had been at IU. His quitting was a great disappointment to many in the valley, and he was treated like something of an outcast when he returned. Though Georgia Bird had not been eager for him to leave home to begin with, her son's decision to quit was still not easy to accept, and for his first month at home she could barely bring herself to speak to him.

Bird himself sometimes wondered if he had blown the only real opportunity of this kind he would ever receive. He enrolled almost immediately at Northwood Institute, a junior college in West Baden, but dropped out just as quickly, disheartened by the low caliber of the basketball played there. He then took a job with the French Lick Street Department, which entailed picking up trash, clearing away snow, repairing roads, mowing grass, and painting benches; he also worked parttime jobs pumping gas and driving a truck.

On February 3, 1975, Joe Bird picked up the phone, called Georgia, said "I want you to hear this," put a shotgun to his head, and pulled the trigger. He had explained to his children beforehand that his suicide was a way of at last doing something positive for his family.

This way, at least, they would receive Social Security payments and veterans benefits.

The death "devastated" Bird, said Jim Jones, though only his mother and Grandmother Kerns were aware of how deeply he was affected; with others he affected his usual laconic stoicism. His fiance, Janet Condra, said that she never heard him speak about his father's death, and she very much doubted that he would have talked about it with anyone else. The only true outward sign of his distress was that he seemed to spend even more time than usual shooting baskets by himself.

Bird decided to return to college—this time at Indiana State, in Terre Haute, where he had really wanted to go all along. "I know what I want out of basketball now. As a 17-year-old, I didn't know," he told a friend. "Indiana State might not be very good right now," Bird said in announcing his decision to attend the school, "but it will be when I get there."

It took Bird little time to feel at home in Terre Haute. Though the city's population was twice that of Bloomington, the student body of Indiana State was only one-third as large as that of IU and was generally less affluent, with fewer out-of-state students. Classes tended to be smaller, and here Bird was less self-conscious about his soft valley twang, rural upbringing, and impoverished background. The presence of two ballplaying buddies from French Lick made him feel more at home as well, and the head basketball coach, Bob King, went out of his way to help him adjust.

As a transfer student, Bird was obligated to sit out of intercollegiate competition for a year, though he could practice with the team. As always, he channeled his frustration into improving his game.

On November 8, 1975, not long after starting at Indiana State, Bird married Janet Condra, his high-school sweetheart. The marriage was a mistake from the start. Janet found her new husband sullen and uncommunicative; Larry, as he grew steadily more confident in himself on the basketball court, seemed to have less of a need for the security that his relationship with Janet had at one time presumably provided. By the time Larry played his first college game, in the autumn of 1976, they were divorced. A very brief reconciliation resulted in the birth of a daughter, Corrie, but by that time the couple had irrevocably split, and Bird was seriously involved with a fellow student at Indiana State, Dinah Mattingly, his current wife, with whom he has had one son, Conor.

By that time as well, the world at large—or at least that part of it that was interested in basketball—was becoming aware of what until then only a few privileged cognoscenti in Terre Haute and the valley had suspected: The best college basketball player in the country was a forgotten, if not totally unknown, 6'9" sophomore forward for the Indiana State Sycamores.

By the new year, the unheralded Sycamores were on a 12-game winning streak and had crashed the top twenty in the nation's basketball polls; Bird had run off 10 straight games in which he scored 40 or more points. At season's end, Indiana State had won 25 games and lost only 2, the best record in its history, and Bird had averaged an almost incomprehensible 32.8 points, 13.3 rebounds, and 4.4 assists per game. Even so, he remained for most of the nation's hoops fans little more than an intriguing rumor, for none of Indiana State's games had been nationally televised and details about him were scarce.

As a junior, Bird was an even better player than the year before. Although his numbers declined slightly, to 30 points, 11.5 rebounds, and 3.9 assists per game, Indiana State had played a significantly tougher schedule—resulting in a relatively disappointing 23 and 9 record—and he was named first team All-American by virtually every important sporting publication. Coaches and commentators marvelled at his unparalleled combination of size and skills: the long-range shooting touch combined with the big man's body, the wizardly passing and dribbling matched with the size, strength, and willingness to bang inside for rebounds, the superlative individual talent married to a commitment to a team concept, the intuitive on-court awareness and intelligence coupled with the physical toughness and reckless ferocity of his play.

Larry Bird, with attorney Bob Woolf, enjoys watching a Celtics game as Red Auerbach (rear) ponders what a steal he's made by drafting Bird a year early.

Because of his family's poverty, many expected Bird to "go hardship," forgo his senior year at Indiana State, and enter the 1978 NBA draft, which was to be held on June 8. But as Bird was happy in Terre Haute and had become quite serious about obtaining his degree, the big money that awaited him in the pros was less of an immediate incentive than most people would have expected. He and his family had always gotten by without much money, he told

In one of the greatest college games ever played, Magic's Spartans were too much for Bird's Sycamores. Here, Jay Vincent and Magic Johnson prevent Bird from getting off a decent shot or pass.

and once again ISU squeezed out a win, 75-74. Though he confessed that his thumb was bothering him, Bird put on one of the most impressive performances in the history of the Final Four, registering 35 points on sizzling 16 for 19 shooting, gathering 16 rebounds, and doling out 9 assists.

Indiana State's narrow victory created the match-up in the championship game that the whole country seemed to have been anticipating. The Michigan State Spartans were led by an outsized, charismatic sophomore point guard named Earvin "Magic" Johnson. Like Bird, with whom he was destined to become forever linked in the memory of appreciative basketball fans, Johnson had led a university team that was a perennial doormat to national prominence; like Bird, he had captured the imagination of basketball fans not so much through his scoring as with his passing.

Bird was the bigger, stronger player and the superior shooter and rebounder, Johnson the faster player and the better ballhandler; both possessed an understanding of the game and commitment to team play that belied their youth and relative inexperience and made them the very rarest of players: the kind who could make their teammates better. The contrast in personalities between the ebullient, outgoing, and joyful Johnson, who reveled in the spotlight, and the tightlipped, remote, and wary Bird, who did everything he could to shun it, only made their match-up that much more intriguing.

The telecast of the 1979 NCAA tournament championship game drew more viewers than any basketball game in the history of televised sports to that point, although the contest itself proved somewhat anticlimactic. Though Bird and Johnson were evenly matched, the Michigan State guard had a much better team, including two future professionals, surrounding him, and the Spartans took control of the game from the outset. At halftime, Michigan State led by 9, and the Spartans ran that advantage to 16 in the second half as the increasingly desperate Bird pleaded with his teammates to "give me the damn ball." At the final buzzer, Michigan State led by 11 and Bird was on the Indiana State bench, sobbing into a towel.

It was a sad ending to an improbable college career, but the intensity of Bird's disappointment only measured how far he had come. The overlooked kid from the valley had led an overmatched bunch of country boys to the national championship game; the confused drop-out had become the unanimous choice as college player of the year (not to mention a college graduate, with a degree in physical education). Never again would anyone express doubt about what Larry Bird could do on the basketball court.

4

SAVING THE LEAGUE

Red Auerbach's gamble paid off. After sometimes difficult negotiations, Bird and the Celtics were able to agree on terms that made him, to that point, the highest-paid rookie in NBA history, and on the court Bird had an impact on his team's fortunes unequaled by any first-year player in NBA history.

In the NBA, the exceptionally rare rookies who had succeeded in immediately transforming their clubs from also-rans to contenders had all been centers: George Mikan, Bill Russell, Wilt Chamberlain, Kareem Abdul-Jabbar, Bill Walton. Good as he might prove to be, there was no reason to believe that Bird, a forward, could singlehandedly lift the Celtics, who had won just 29 games (out of 82) in 1978-79, back into the championship hunt.

But Bird was a unique talent. For one thing, because of his one-year layoff, he was almost a year older than the average rookie, and that

Larry Bird was not the most graceful of players, but he did whatever it took to win.

much more mature physically and mentally. Though some had predicted that he would experience adjustment problems similar to those he had undergone in Bloomington, he immediately earned the respect of his teammates with his unassuming personality and desire to fit in off the court, and his confident and unselfish play on it. His game, of course, was by now fully matured and required very few adjustments to it on the professional level.

With Bird's passing inspiring a team commitment to unselfish play—"To Larry, winning is the most important thing, whether he has to shoot, pass, or rebound to do it," Auerbach said—the Celtics finished first in their division, winning 61 of their 82 games, the best record in the league and the greatest one-season turnaround in the history of the NBA. There was little doubt that Bird was the primary reason for the improbable 32-game improvement, for aside from him, there had been no significant changes to the Boston roster.

For the season, Bird averaged 21.3 points, 10.4 rebounds, and 4.5 assists per game. Though Magic Johnson was enjoying almost as spectacular a debut with the Los Angeles Lakers, Bird was the near unanimous choice for the league's rookie-of-the year award, polling 63 of the 66 votes. He also finished third in the MVP voting, behind only Abdul-Jabbar and Julius Erving.

The only disappointing part of Bird's rookie campaign was the Celtics' elimination in the Eastern Conference finals, in a surprisingly easy five games, by their archrivals, the Philadelphia 76ers, who had finished two games behind them in the regular season.

Philadelphia then went on to lose in the championship series to Johnson and Abdul-Jabbar's Lakers, with Magic putting on one of the alltime great playoff performances in the series' final game. In championships, at least, Magic was still up on Bird, who acknowledged that a real sense of rivalry existed between them. "Even then [before their NCAA championship game clash], I sensed it," Bird said before the first regular-season match-up of his Celtics and Magic's Lakers. "I knew that whatever team he played for and whatever team I played for were going to be battling for whatever's there."

Bird and Johnson revitalized not only their teams but the league as well. At the time they entered the league, the NBA was having almost as difficult a time of it as were the Celtics. Television ratings were down drastically, as was arena attendance; several franchises were in imminent danger of folding, and the drop-off in fan interest was so severe that there were serious doubts about the NBA's future viability.

Rightly or wrongly, many observers associated the NBA's image problems with its changing racial composition. By the time Bird and Johnson entered the NBA, almost 80 percent of the league's players were black; the vast majority of American society, including the audience for professional sports, remained white, of course, and the great unanswered question that hung over the league was whether that audience would patronize so predominantly black a sport.

Bird, though he always resisted such characterizations as implicitly racist, was hailed as the "great white hope" the league supposedly needed to retain the interest of white fans, although it was his game and legendary work ethic that were even more critical than his skin color in redefining the way the NBA was perceived. Interestingly, this great white hope had always indentified more with black players than with their white counterparts, mainly because the impoverished backgrounds from which so many black players came more closely resembled his own. In consistently shunning the role of white savior, he always refuted the prevailing stereotypes about white and black players, insisting that blacks dominated the game because they were "hungrier" and worked harder. "It's a black man's game," he said on many occasions. "I just try to fit in."

Even in their most glorious days of the 1960s, when they won nine championships in 10 years, the Celtics had had trouble selling tickets, but with Bird the team enjoyed a streak of consecutive home-game sellouts that lasted more than a decade. "Bird has sold more tickets, as an individual attraction throughout this league, than any player before him," Auerbach said. Johnson proved no less popular, and together

Bird played tenacious defense against Julius Erving in the 1980 playoffs, but Philadelphia won anyway.

the two newcomers sparked an unprecedented explosion of interest in professional basketball, one that ushered in what is now recognized as the golden age of the NBA. During their first 10 years in the league, attendance increased by 26 percent, television revenue by 450 percent, and gross revenue by more than 100 percent.

Bird's statement that "I knew whatever team [Johnson] was playing for and whatever team I was playing for were going to be battling for whatever's there" proved prophetic. Either his Celtics or Johnson's Lakers played for the championship in every year of the 1980s; in three of those years, they squared off against each other.

After the Lakers won the championship in 1980, the Celtics got a chance to even the score. With a revamped front line that included new acquisitions Robert Parish and Kevin McHale, the Celtics won 62 games. Though Bird's second-year statistics indicated only a slight improvement on his part, he received thunderous acclaim for his performance. In his own words, Bird considered himself a "dumb hick," but Houston Rockets guard Robert Reid summed up the general feeling of Bird's competitors: "He's the smartest player I've played against."

Bird finished second to Erving in the 1981 MVP voting, but he thoroughly outplayed the Philadelphia forward in the 76ers-Celtics rematch in the conference finals. Philadelphia jumped out to a three games to one lead. Bird remained confident, even though the Celtics had to play once more in Philadelphia, where they had lost 11 straight games, and even though in NBA history a team had successfully

Bird accepts the cheers after the 1981 NBA championship. To his right is Celtic's coach K. C. Jones.

rallied from such a deficit just three times in 67 occurrences.

Boston won games five and six, each by the margin of a single basket. The seventh and deciding contest was "the most emotional" game he has ever played in, Bird later said; the last five minutes were also the most unrelentingly physical basketball he had ever experienced. With the score tied and just over a minute to play in the seventh and deciding contest, Philadelphia's Darryl Dawkins missed a critical shot, and Bird emerged with the rebound from the scramble of desperately straining players under the Boston basket. He headed straight upcourt with the basketball, uncharacteristically not even considering the notion of a pass. "There was no place in the world I wanted that ball except in my hands," he said afterwards. With the 76ers in full retreat, Bird pulled up about 17 feet from the hoop, just left of the foul circle, and banked in a leaning jump shot. "I hate to bank shots," he remembered in *Drive*. "Why I decided to bank that one I'll never know." However inexplicable the rationale behind it, the shot won the game—and the series—for the Celtics.

He was no less dominating against the Houston Rockets, Boston's opponent in the finals, as he led both teams in rebounds, assists, and steals. The Rockets got an inkling of what they were in for in the fourth quarter of the very first game, when Bird turned in one of the single most memorable plays of his high-light-filled career: Having launched a 22-foot jumper, he recognized immediately that the shot was off and, moreover, that it would carom long to the right near the endline. He immediately sprinted toward the spot, catching the ball in midflight, and, as his momentum carried him over the baseline and out of bounds, switched the ball from his right to his left hand and flipped it through the hoop from about 12 feet away.

The play defied description, but, composed of equal parts hustle, ingenuity, and athletic ability, it defined Bird's game.

In game six, with Houston rallying and Boston nursing a rapidly dwindling three-point lead, Bird took a pass deep along the left baseline, quickly reckoned his position on the floor, nervily took one step back beyond the three-point line, and let fly. The ball hit nothing but net, and the Rockets were done. With Boston's championship came unanimous acknowledgment of Bird's stature as a player. "I don't think there's ever been a better player in the league than Larry," said Chicago Bulls assistant coach Jerry Sloan.

5
THE LEGEND

If, as Sloan and many others like him insisted, Bird was already, at this stage in his young professional career, the best player in the NBA, it did not stop him from his usual dedication to self-improvement. Summers were spent back home in the valley (where he built a home for himself and his mother) fine-tuning his game, and during the season the first arrivals at the Celtics early-morning practices were no longer surprised to discover Bird asleep upon the gymnasium mats, napping after a nocturnal workout. His individual pregame practice sessions were already the stuff of NBA legend: hours before gametime, long before the first fans and even some of his teammates would have arrived in the arena, Bird would appear on the court to shoot for a long time by himself. It was as if his memories of the hardscrabble days in the valley were never far out of his

The referees had to separate Bird and Kareem Abdul-Jabbar in the fourth game of the 1984 playoffs.

mind, still pushing him. "It's like I get this guilty feeling that I'm not playing enough, that someone somewhere is playing more," he told a reporter.

Though such dedication resulted in measurable improvement in Bird's already exquisite game—in 1982 and then 1983, he recorded new career highs in points, rebounds, assists, and field-goal percentage to finish second in the MVP voting each year to Moses Malone—the Celtics as a team could not keep pace with him. In 1982, Boston was ousted from the conference finals after a 63-win regular season by the Philadelphia 76ers, who were in turn defeated for the championship by the Lakers, and the following season the Celtics slumped to only 56 wins and were swept, shockingly, in the second round of the playoffs by the Milwaukee Bucks.

For the next five years, Larry Bird played basketball at a whole new level. Over that time, he would average almost 28 points, 10 rebounds, and 7 assists per game, while carrying the Celtics to an average of 62 regular season wins, five division crowns, four NBA finals, and two NBA championships. For three years consecutively, from 1984 to 1986, he would be voted the league's most valuable player, becoming the first non-center in history to win three MVPs, let alone in succession. During that same time, he would become only the fourth player in history to win both the regular-season and playoff MVP in the same year, and the only player to achieve that particular distinction twice.

For fans of the NBA, these years were perhaps most memorable for the now legendary championship-round matchups between Bird's

Bill Walton and Larry Bird sandwich Houston's star, Hakeem Olajuwon. The Celtics went on to win the 1986 championship.

Celtics and Johnson's Lakers. The first (and for Bird the most satisfying) of these showdowns took place in 1984.

"Me and Larry at last" was how Johnson succinctly summarized the anticipation with which basketball fans looked forward to the series, which was watched by the largest television audience ever to watch an NBA championship series. The two rivals stood unchallenged, except by one another, as the only conceivable nominees for the title of best all-around player in the game, and there seemed no better way to determine a winner to the eternal disputes over which was truly the better player than a playoff series for the NBA championship.

Initially, the advantage seemed to be Johnson's, as the Lakers, with their celebrated "Showtime" fast break working to near perfection, steamrolled the Celtics in two of the series' first three games. But then Bird spoke up. "We played like sissies. . . . I can't believe a team like this would let LA come out and push us around the way they did," he said of himself and his teammates before game four, and the whole tenor of the series changed. Now, there were far fewer easy Los Angeles baskets; each time a Laker went to the hoop, a Celtic was there to challenge him. The defining moment came when Kevin McHale, trailing the Lakers' Kurt Rambis on a fast break, clotheslined the Los Angeles forward and sent him flying into one of the basket supports. The foul was in flagrant disregard of the letter and spirit of the NBA rulebook, but it delivered a clear message: Showtime was over. If the Lakers wanted to go to the hoop, they were going to be challenged—hard—every time. Moments later, Bird went toe to toe in a shouting match with Abdul-Jabbar after an exchange of elbows.

Boston's physical approach had the desired effect. "Before," said Celtics forward Cedric Maxwell, "the Lakers were just running across the street whenever they wanted. Now, they stop at the corner, push the button, wait for the light, and look both ways." Even so, it took a typically clutch Bird performance to keep Boston alive. With 16 seconds remaining, he hit two foul shots to tie the game and send it into overtime. In the extra period, again with just ticks left on the clock and the score still tied, he posted up Magic in the lane for a turn-around jumper that proved to be the game-winner.

For the series, Bird averaged 27 points and 14 rebounds per game and easily enjoyed the best of his speculative (the two players rarely actually guarded each other) match-up with Johnson, whose uncharacteristic and costly late-game miscues had likely cost his team the title. Even Los Angeles general manager Jerry West conceded that at this point in their careers, Bird was the better player. "Bird whets your appetite for the game," West said. "He's such a great passer, and he doesn't make mis-takes. Magic handles the ball more and he makes more mistakes because he has it more.... The one who best approaches the kind of player I would recommend a young player model him-self after is Bird. He's a genius on the floor."

Meanness and genius were both in evidence during Bird's 1985-86 season, sometimes on the same night. The Boston-Philadelphia rivalry was second in intensity only to that of the Celtics and the Lakers, and Bird's match-ups with the universally-revered Julius "Doctor J" Erving were nearly as ballyhooed as his show-downs with Johnson. Early in the year, while in the process of outscoring the hallowed Erving 42 points to 6, Bird's trashtalking—he had become, by consensus, the league's champion in that category—so infuriated the usually reserved and dignified Doctor that he resorted to fisticuffs, and both players were ejected. "Hey, I could be a nice guy, too," Bird told his head coach, K. C. Jones. "I just don't have the time. There are games to be won."

And Boston was winning more of them—63—than any team in the league. At times, Bird's dominance on the court was so complete that he confessed to growing bored and to attempting something spectacularly difficult simply to see if it could be done. At one point in the season, he won two consecutive games for Boston with shots at the final buzzer; when Kevin McHale set a Celtics single-game record of 56 points, Bird, who often upbraided McHale for what he regarded as a lackadaisical approach to the game, told his fellow forward that he should have scored more if he wanted the record to stand for more than a couple of days. Just nine days later, Bird threw in 60 against Atlanta—including 32 in one particularly torrid 14-minute stretch—in a performance so incandescent that it had even the Hawks benchwarmers high-fiving each other and waving towels in appreciation. "I mean, it was *frightening*," Dennis Johnson said. "Everything he touched, he threw in like a guided missile, from no matter where. First, we were laughing, then we were in shock."

Though Bird enjoyed a truly sensational year, lifting his per game average nearly five points a game, to a career-best 28.7, his willingness to use his fists came back to haunt him after he injured his right index finger in a barroom fight during the Eastern Conference playoffs. Hampered already by a bad back and an injured elbow, he shot poorly in the championship rematch with the Lakers, who claimed the crown.

The next season, however, the Celtics and

Magic Johnson once wrote, "Whenever [the Lakers] play the Celtics, it seems like we're playing in the last game that'll be played in basketball history." Here Bird ducks around Lakers center Kareem Abdul-Jabbar, as Danny Ainge (left) looks on and Robert Parish (right) trails on the play.

Bird were back with one of the best teams of all time. With their bench strengthened by the addition of hall-of-fame–bound Bill Walton, Boston won 67 games, the third-best record in league history, and swept through the playoffs to a six-game defeat of the Houston Rockets for their third and last championship of the Bird years. Although Bird started the season slowly, hindered by the back problems that would ulti-mately end his career, he came on strong to capture the Most Valuable Player award for both the regular season and the playoffs. Indeed, by season's end, the intensity with which he was playing was almost frightening. "I got more psyched up for this series [in which he averaged 24 points, 10 rebounds, and 10 assists per game] than any I've ever played in," he said about the games with the Rockets, whose forward Jim Peterson testified to the effects of Bird's determination. "I never saw anyone demoralize a team the way Larry did," said Peterson. "I saw him take on five guys by himself. At times, he doesn't need teammates."

If, for Bird, anything had been lacking in his 1986 season, it was that the campaign had not ended against the Lakers. In their eighth year in the league, both he and Johnson had come to recognize that they had only the other as the standard against which to measure their own excellence. "Larry Bird is the only player I fear," Johnson had said on more than one occasion. "Magic is the only player who understands the game the way I do," Bird said. Over time, mutu-al admiration of each other's play had led to a friendship so close that Johnson likened it to a marriage, and they had begun to talk of retiring at the same time at some point in the future, unable to imagine finding a challenge equal to what they and their teams posed to one another.

The two met for the last time in the playoffs in the 1987 championship series. Even before the series began, there were signs that a chang-ing of the guard was taking place. Though Bird had enjoyed a customarily superb regular sea-son, his back troubled him more than ever

before, and it was Johnson, not him, who had
been voted the league's most valuable player.
Then the Celtics had barely, with the help of
Bird's miraculous steal of Thomas's inbounds
pass, held off in seven games the young
Pistons, who were obviously the coming power
in the Eastern Conference. It seemed likely that
for Bird and the Celtics the glory days were
nearing an end.

The first two games of the series with the
Lakers did nothing to dispel that impression, as
Los Angeles, fast breaking on nearly every pos-
session, almost ran the Celtics right off the
floorboards of the Los Angeles Forum in registering two easy triumphs. The defending cham-
pions looked old and tired, as if they did not
even belong on the same court with the Lakers.

But with three straight games at home, the
Celtics still had a chance to climb back into the
series. Taking a page from 1984, Bird criticized
his team's lackluster approach. The Celtics
needed "twelve heart transplants," he said, and
for almost 96 minutes it seemed like Bird's
timely cajoling and inspired play might create
another Boston miracle. Behind his 30 points,
the Celtics took game three by six, and his
clutch three-point shot from deep in the corner
had his team ahead by a point with just eight
seconds remaining in game four. But Magic,
atoning at last for his costly miscues in 1984,
buried a 14-foot "junior, junior skyhook" over
Parish and McHale with two seconds remaining
to put Los Angeles in front; when Bird missed a
desperation three-pointer at the buzzer, Los
Angeles had an insurmountable three games to
one lead, and the Lakers went on to wrap up
the series at home in game six. At the press

Bird calls the play as Dominique Wilkins guards him. In one of his greatest performances, Bird shot 10 for 11 in the fourth quarter of the seventh game and almost singlehandedly beat the Atlanta Hawks to move on in the 1988 playoffs.

conference following the series finale, Bird shook his head ruefully. "Magic's the best," he said in his soft Indiana twang. "He's the best I've ever seen. He's a perfect basketball player."

If Bird's comments sounded a little like a concession speech, in some ways they were. Three years younger than he, Magic was just entering his athletic prime, while Bird was just exiting his. At 30, the beginning of athletic old age (particularly for an NBA player), Bird was beginning to feel the effects of all the numerous injuries and aches—the bad back, sprains and tears in his ankles and feet, an arthritic elbow, a broken cheekbone, and numerous others—he had played through. "I have never had an athlete in my 39 years in the league who liked to play more than Larry does and who would make every effort to play whether he was hurt or not," Red Auerbach said, but that dedication had taken its toll on Bird in his eight years in the league, during which he had logged more regular season minutes than any other player in the league. He had also during that time played in more playoff games than any other player, which only added to the wear and tear on his body.

There was still some great basketball to come, but his best days were behind him. Bird averaged a career-best 29.9 points per game in 1988, but that year also marked the ninth and last time he would be named to the All-NBA first team. In the fourth quarter of the seventh game of the second round of the playoffs, he turned in one of his greatest and most famous performances, hitting 10 of 11 shots and making the game's key defensive plays to outduel the Atlanta Hawks' almost equally scintillating Dominique Wilkins and lift Boston to a two-point victory. Auerbach called it the greatest quarter he had ever seen, but it was something of a last hurrah; against the Pistons in the conference finals, Bird, who had been playing with a bad case of pneumonia, was virtually shut down by Dennis Rodman, and Detroit won in six.

The loss marked the effective end of the Celtics dynasty; aside from Bird, the three other most important Celtics—Parish, McHale, and Johnson—were all on the downside of their careers, and the team would never again

In the last years of his career, Bird's aching back often forced him to lie on the ground on the sidelines.

advance as far in the playoffs during what remained of Bird's career. Detroit was now the dominant power in the East; the Pistons would play in the finals the next three years, winning in 1989 and 1990. Magic would win the MVP Award in 1989 and 1990, but even the Lakers' time was drawing to a close; the championship they won in 1988 would be their last, and for the five years afterward it would be the Pistons and the Chicago Bulls flaunting their championship rings. When people talked about the best player in the game, the name most often mentioned would be Michael Jordan.

After just six games of the 1988-89 season, Bird underwent surgery to repair bone spurs on both ankles. The spurs had been bothering him for six years; at times, he said, it felt as if someone was twisting a knife inside both his Achilles tendons, and some days it was painful for him just to stand up. He did not play again that season; when he returned in 1989-90, it was clear that he was not the same player. Though still first-rate, he was not vintage Bird; his mobility was severely limited, and he became much more of a post-up player and stand-up jump shooter than he had ever been. His worsening back problems limited him to 60 games in 1991, when for the first time in his career his scoring average dipped below 20 points per game, and, following surgery, to just 45 games in 1992.

But even as Bird's physical abilities diminished, his understanding of the game seemed only to deepen, and his passing grew more brilliantly conceived than ever; for basketball purists there was a great delight in watching him operate out of the low post, back arched both to maintain a distance from the defender and to feel his whereabouts, always talking some classic trash, and, with a quick flip over his shoulder or a backhand bounce pass off one of his hips to a cutting teammate, demonstrate the truth of the basketball axiom that it is less important how you move than how the ball moves. Finally, in the summer of 1992, Bird surrendered to the inevitable, and after earning a gold medal at the Olympics as a member (with such fellow stars as Johnson, Jordan, and Charles Barkley) of the so-called U.S. Dream Team, he announced his retirement from the game that had given his life so much meaning. At a special ceremony held to honor him the following season, his white jersey with the green trim, bearing the famous number 33, was hoisted to the rafters of the Boston Garden, there to flutter alongside the retired uniforms of past Celtic immortals. As an admiring Magic Johnson once tried to explain, "to other players basketball is a job. To Larry Bird, basketball is *his life.*"

STATISTICS

LARRY JOE BIRD
(Boston Celtics)

SEASON	G	MIN	FGA	FGM	PCT	FTA	FTM	PCT	RBD	AST	PTS	AVG
1979–80	82	2955	1463	693	.474	360	301	.836	852	370	1745	21.3
1980–81	82	3239	1503	719	.478	328	283	.863	895	451	1741	21.2
1981–82	77	2923	1414	711	.503	380	328	.863	837	447	1761	22.9
1982–83	79	2982	1481	747	.504	418	351	.840	870	348	1867	23.6
1983–84	79	3028	1542	758	.492	421	374	**.888**	796	520	1908	24.2
1984–85	80	3161	1760	918	.522	457	403	.882	842	531	2295	28.7
1985–86	82	3113	1606	796	.496	492	441	**.896**	805	557	2115	25.8
1986–87	74	3005	1497	786	.525	455	414	**.910**	682	566	2076	28.1
1987–88	76	2965	1672	881	.527	453	415	.916	703	467	2276	29.9
1988–89	8	189	104	49	.471	19	18	.947	37	29	116	19.3
1989–90	75	2944	1517	718	.473	343	319	**.930**	712	562	1820	24.3
1990–91	60	2277	1017	462	.454	183	163	.891	509	431	1164	19.4
1991–92	45	1662	758	353	.466	162	150	.926	434	306	908	20.2

Totals

	G	MIN	FGA	FGM	PCT	FTA	FTM	PCT	RBD	AST	PTS	AVG
	897	34443	17334	8591	.496	4471	3960	.886	8974	5695	21791	24.3

Playoff Totals

	G	MIN	FGA	FGM	PCT	FTA	FTM	PCT	RBD	AST	PTS	AVG
	164	6886	3090	1458	.472	1012	901	.890	1683	1062	3897	23.8

All-Star Totals

	G	MIN	FGA	FGM	PCT	FTA	FTM	PCT	RBD	AST	PTS	AVG
	10	287	123	52	.423	32	27	.844	79	41	134	13.4

G	games
MIN	minutes
FGA	field goals attempted
FGM	field goals made
PCT	percent
FTA	free throws attempted
FTM	free throws made
RBD	rebounds
AST	assists
PTS	points
AVG	scoring average

bold indicates league-leading figures

LARR[Y BIRD]
A CHR[ONOLOGY]

Larry Bird a chronology.

1956   Born Larry Joe Bird on Dec[...]

1974   Averages more than 30 poi[nts...]
Springs Valley but fails to b[...]
team; accepts scholarship t[...]
24 days

1975   Joe Bird, Larry's father, con[...]ol
and accepts scholarship to Indiana State University; marries Janet
Condra, high school sweetheart

1976   Divorces Condra; plays first college game

1977   Averages more than 32 points and 13 rebounds per game in leading
Indiana State to the best record in its history

1978   Selected first-team All-American; forgoes declaring hardship in NBA draft
yet is selected by the Boston Celtics as the sixth pick overall

1979   Selected first-team All-American and college player of the year; leads
Indiana State to undefeated regular season record and the championship
game of the NCAA tournament, where they are defeated by Magic
Johnson's Michigan State team

1980   Wins NBA Rookie of the Year Award in leading Boston to the greatest one-
season turnaround in NBA history to that point

1981   Leads Boston to the NBA championship

1984   Wins first of record-setting three consecutive Most Valuable Player
Awards; Boston defeats Los Angeles for the NBA crown

1986   Wins third straight MVP Award; Boston wins its third and last NBA championship of the "Bird era"

1987   Plays in championship round for final time against Los Angeles and Magic
Johnson

1988   Records career high in scoring; named All-NBA first team for ninth (and
final) consecutive time

1989   Surgery on feet limits him to just six games

1992   Selected to All-Star team for 12th year (out of 13 seasons); wins gold
medal as member of U.S. Olympic team; announces retirement after three
seasons of reduced effectiveness because of injuries

SUGGESTIONS FOR FURTHER READING

Bird, Larry with Bob Ryan. *Bird: The Story of My Life*. New York: Doubleday, 1990.

Frank, Steven. *Magic Johnson*. New York: Chelsea House, 1995.

George, Nelson. *Elevating the Game*. New York: HarperCollins, 1993.

Johnson, Earvin, Jr. with Roy S. Johnson. *Magic's Touch*. New York: Addison-Wesley, 1990.

Levine, Lee Daniel. *Bird: The Making of an American Sports Legend*. New York: McGraw Hill, 1988.

Ryan, Bob, and Dick Raphael. *The Boston Celtics*. New York: Addison-Wesley, 1989.

INDEX

ABOUT THE AUTHOR

Sean Dolan has a degree in literature and American history from the State University of New York. He is the author of many biographies and histories for young adult readers, including *Michael Jordan* in the Black Americans of Achievement Series.